NINJA

ANDREW JENNINGS

BLOOMSBURY EDUCATION

LONDON   OXFORD   NEW YORK   NEW DELHI   SYDNEY

BLOOMSBURY EDUCATION

Bloomsbury Publishing Plc

50 Bedford Square, London, WC1B 3DP, UK

29 Earlsfort Terrace, Dublin 2, Ireland

BLOOMSBURY, BLOOMSBURY EDUCATION and the Diana logo are trademarks of Bloomsbury Publishing Plc

First published in 2021, UK, by Bloomsbury Education

Text copyright © Andrew Jennings, 2021

'Exciting Sentences' section © Alan Peat, 2021

Illustrations copyright © Shutterstock

A catalogue record for this book is available from the British Library

ISBN: PB: 978-1-4729-8830-0; ePDF: 978-1-4729-8831-7; ePub: 978-1-4729-8829-4

6 8 10 9 7 5

Text design by Jeni Child

Printed and bound in the UK by CPI Group Ltd, Croydon CR0 4YY

To find out more about our authors and books visit www.bloomsbury.com and sign up for our newsletters

Contents

Contents continued...

1 Grammar essentials

ADJECTIVES

Adjectives are words that are used to describe people, objects and places: in most instances, nouns. Adjectives add detail. So rather than, 'the tree', you could say, 'the **tall** tree'. You can combine one, two or even three adjectives. These would be separated by a comma, for example, 'the **tall, ancient** tree'.

Adjectives (a–c)

- abrupt
- acidic
- adorable
- adventurous
- aggressive
- agitated

- alert
- aloof
- bored
- brave
- bright
- colossal

- condescending
- confused
- cooperative
- corny
- costly
- courageous

Adjectives (d-g)

* despicable
* determined
* dilapidated
* diminutive
* distressed
* disturbed
* exasperated
* excited
* exhilarated
* extensive
* exuberant
* foolish

* frantic
* fresh
* friendly
* frightened
* frothy
* frustrating
* funny
* fuzzy
* gaudy
* glorious
* graceful
* greasy
* grieving
* gritty
* grotesque
* grubby
* grumpy

Adjectives (h-z)

handsome
happy
healthy
helpful
helpless
high
hollow
homely
hungry
hurt
icy
ideal
immense
impressionable

intrigued
irate
large
livid
lonely
loose
lovely
lucky
mysterious
narrow
nasty
outrageous
panicky
perfect

perplexed
teeny
tender
tense
terrible
tricky
troubled
unsightly
upset
vile
wicked
yummy
zany
zippy

SUPERLATIVES

Superlatives are another useful tool for describing and comparing. Superlatives compare and describe to the greatest degree. For example, the man was not just angry, he was the **angriest** man. This helps us show just how angry he is.

Superlatives (a-f)

angriest	chewiest	curliest
biggest	chubbiest	deadliest
blackest	classiest	dirtiest
blandest	cleanest	dullest
bloodiest	cleverest	earliest
boldest	cloudiest	easiest
bossiest	clumsiest	faintest
bravest	coldest	fewest
brightest	creamiest	filthiest
busiest	creepiest	flakiest
cheapest	crunchiest	funniest

Superlatives (g-z)

- gentlest
- gloomiest
- grandest
- gravest
- greasiest
- greatest
- greediest
- healthiest
- heaviest
- highest
- hungriest
- itchiest

- juiciest
- kindest
- laziest
- loneliest
- loudest
- moistest
- narrowest
- nicest
- oddest
- prettiest
- proudest
- purest
- quietest
- rarest
- richest
- ripest
- roomiest

- roughest
- rudest
- safest
- scariest
- shallowest
- shiniest
- simplest
- skinniest
- smelliest
- smoothest
- strangest
- strictest
- truest
- weirdest
- windiest
- worthiest
- youngest

VERBS

Verbs are very important words. They help us describe how a character or object is acting or behaving. Verb choices can help the reader understand exactly how an event, action or behaviour is happening.

Here are some common verbs. Pages 11 – 13 have even more verbs to try.

Common verbs

- add
- allow
- bake
- bang
- call
- chase
- damage
- drop
- end
- escape
- fasten
- fix

- gather
- hang
- hug
- imagine
- itch
- jog
- jump
- kick
- knit
- land
- lock
- march

- mix
- name
- notice
- obey
- open
- pass
- promise
- question
- reach
- rinse
- scatter
- stay

- talk
- turn
- untie
- use
- vanish
- visit
- walk
- work
- yawn
- yell
- zip
- zoom

More verbs (a-d)

admire	cascade	deal
adore	cast	deceive
alter	catapult	declare
amble	cherish	demand
amuse	cleave	design
announce	comment	desire
arrive	conceal	despise
ascend	confound	deter
assault	confuse	devour
bargain	conspire	digest
bellow	corrupt	dine
blabber	craft	disarm
bluster	crave	dismantle
boast	create	drain
bolt	creep	dwell
brew	dawdle	
burrow	dazzle	

More verbs (e – m)

encourage	gloat	journey
enjoy	gorge	laugh
evolve	guffaw	lament
excite	gush	leach
exhaust	halt	liquefy
exit	howl	loaf
extract	huff	loathe
float	hurl	lob
flounce	ignite	lope
flow	implore	lounge
follow	impress	manipulate
forbid	inhale	manufacture
gasp	inquire	meander
gaze	instruct	modify
gel	insult	morph
glide	jab	mount

More verbs (n – z)

- neglect
- nibble
- nudge
- occupy
- ooze
- outrage
- overrule
- pacify
- peek
- peer
- persuade
- petrify
- plead
- plot
- poke
- prod
- pursue

- relish
- require
- ruin
- saunter
- scale
- scoff
- scurry
- shriek
- sigh
- sink
- slurp
- smudge
- snap
- snicker
- snuffle
- spatter
- spew

- sprinkle
- squeal
- stagger
- stalk
- startle
- stride
- stroke
- stroll
- treasure
- venture
- wander
- wish

ADVERBS

Where a verb tells us what is happening, adverbs give a greater level of detail about how the action or behaviour is happening. For example, 'the man was running', could be enhanced by, 'the man was running **awkwardly**'.

* accidentally
* actually
* acutely
* always
* annually
* anxiously
* arrogantly
* awkwardly
* beautifully
* bitterly
* bravely
* briefly
* carefully
* certainly
* daily
* doubtfully
* easily

* especially
* exactly
* fairly
* generally
* greatly
* happily
* helplessly
* honestly
* immediately
* jealously
* keenly
* loudly
* miserably
* mysteriously
* naturally
* officially
* often

* politely
* quickly
* randomly
* rapidly
* regularly
* seldom
* slowly
* smoothly
* suddenly
* thankfully
* unexpectedly
* unfortunately
* usefully
* voluntarily
* wrongly
* yesterday
* zealously

FRONTED ADVERBIALS

Fronted adverbials are used for beginning sentences by focusing on location, time, frequency, manner or the degree in which something is happening. They are great for helping the reader visualise or sequence what is occurring in the writing.

Location

Above me,

Around the corner,

Close by,

Downstairs,

Here,

In my heart,

In the crowd,

In the distance,

Inside,

Inside the box,

Inside the woods,

Nearby,

Next to the _____,

Outside,

Outside the building,

Standing by the river,

Underneath me,

Under the bridge,

Upstairs,

15

Time

After a while,
Afterwards,
All of a sudden,
Already,
Always,
As soon as I finish,
At lunch time,
Before long,
Before they left,
Eventually,
Immediately,
In the morning,
Last month,
Later,
Later on,
Later today,
Next year,
Now,
Soon,
Today,
Tomorrow,
Yesterday,

Frequency

Again,
Always,
Constantly,
Daily,
Fortnightly,
Frequently,
Hourly,
Infrequently,
Monthly,
Never,
Never before,
Often,
Once,
Rarely,
Regularly,
Sometimes,
Twice,
Weekly,
Yearly,

Manner

Anxiously,

As quick as a flash,

Awkwardly,

Bravely,

Carefully,

Cautiously,

Curiously,

Frantically,

Happily,

Infamously,

Noisily,

Presumptuously,

Quietly,

Rapidly,

Reluctantly,

Sadly,

Sickeningly,

Silently,

Sneakily,

Suddenly,

Without moving,

Unwittingly,

Degree

Almost dead,

Breathing heavily,

Brimming with excitement,

Bursting to start,

Close to tears,

Completely starving,

Extremely unimpressed,

Full of joy,

Half asleep,

Overwhelmed with relief,

Totally confused,

Totally overwhelmed,

Unbearably brave,

Under the influence,

CONJUNCTIONS

Coordinating conjunctions

Coordinating conjunctions help us join two clauses together. A clause is a complete thought and it normally contains a subject and a verb. A good way to remember your coordinating conjunctions is the acronym **FANBOYS**.

F	for
A	and
N	nor
B	but
O	or
Y	yet
S	so

Subordinating conjunctions

Subordinating conjunctions introduce subordinate clauses, which also normally contain a subject and a verb. Subordinate clauses depend on a main clause to make sense. They can sometimes be used to begin a sentence to help vary your sentence structure.

after	if	than
although	in order that	that
as	in case	though
as if	in the event that	till
as long as	lest	unless
as much as	meanwhile	until
as soon as	now that	when
as though	once	whenever
because	only	where
before	only if	whereas
by the time	provided that	wherever
even if	since	whether or not
even though	so	while
however	supposing	

MODAL VERBS

Modal verbs are used to suggest how likely, probable or possible something is. If you say, 'I will call later', the modal verb 'will' suggests that it is very likely to happen.

* can / can't
* could / couldn't
* may / may not
* might / mightn't
* must / mustn't
* ought to / ought not to
* shall / shan't / shall not
* should / shouldn't
* will / won't
* would / wouldn't

DETERMINERS

Determiners help the reader understand if we are referring to one object (singular), more than one (plural) or exactly what it is that we are referring to.

Articles: a, an, the

Possessives: my, your, his, her, its, our, their, whose

Demonstratives: this, that, these, those

Numbers: one, two, three, four, five, six...

Ordinal numbers: first, second, third, fourth, fifth, sixth...

Quantifiers: a few, a lot, another, any, many, much, several, some, very

PRONOUNS

Pronouns are useful because they help us to avoid repeating nouns over and over again. This can be annoying for the reader. For example, rather than saying 'Mark and Rohan' many times over, you might use, 'they', 'the boys' or 'the pair'.

Personal pronouns

* I, me, my, mine, myself
* you, your, yours, yourself
* he, him, his, himself
* she, her, hers, herself
* it, its, itself

* we, us, our, ours, ourselves
* you, your, yours, yourselves
* they, them, their, theirs, themselves

Relative pronouns

Relative pronouns are words that allow you to introduce a relative clause. Relative clauses are a type of subordinate clause, meaning they contain a subject and verb but still require a main clause to make complete sense. They are great for adding detail.

- that
- what
- when
- where
- which
- who
- whose

FORMAL AND INFORMAL LANGUAGE

Formal language is used in more official writing, such as when you write a letter or a balanced argument. Normally, we use formal language to show that we are serious.

Informal language is often used in more relaxed situations, where conversation happens between friends or people who know each other. Informal language can include contractions (see page 24).

Formal – Informal

absent – off

allow – let

apologise – say sorry

appear – seem

cancel – end

children – kids

choose – pick

combat – fight

consider – think about

construct – build

consume – eat

damage – break

demonstrate – show

discard – throw away

disclose – tell

Formal – Informal

ancient – old

begin – start

desire – want

enquire – ask

evade – avoid

fortunate – lucky

incorrect – wrong

injure – hurt

quit – give up

request – ask

resilient – tough

support – help

terminate – end

verify – check

without – lack

23

CONTRACTIONS

'Contract' means 'shorten or shrink'. Contractions are where two words are joined together to form a single word with an apostrophe. To shorten the word, certain letters are removed (the apostrophe takes this place). Contractions can be used to show informal language (see page 23).

are not	aren't	is not	isn't	we are	we're
can not	can't	it will	it'll	we had	we'd
could not	couldn't	must not	mustn't	we have	we've
did not	didn't	she had	she'd	we will	we'll
does not	doesn't	she has	she's	we would	we'd
do not	don't	she will	she'll	were not	weren't
had not	hadn't	she would	she'd	what is	what's
have not	haven't	should not	shouldn't	where is	where's
he had	he'd	that is	that's	who is	who's
he will	he'll	there is	there's	who will	who'll
he would	he'd	they are	they're	will not	won't
here is	here's	they had	they'd	would not	wouldn't
I am	I'm	they have	they've	you are	you're
I have	I've	they will	they'll	you had	you'd
I will	I'll	they would	they'd	you will	you'll
		was not	wasn't	you would	you'd

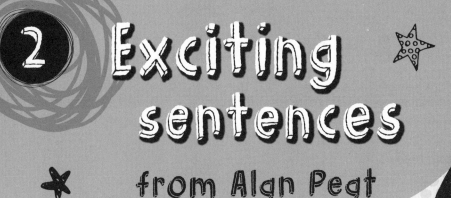

Exciting sentences
from Alan Peat

BOYS – but, or, yet, so

A *BOYS* sentence has two parts. The first part always ends with a comma and the second part always begins with a coordinating conjunction. The most popular coordinating conjunctions are:

↓ **B** but   ↓ **O** or   ↓ **Y** yet   ↓ **S** so

Examples

* She was a strict woman most of the time, **but** she could be kind.

* He could be really friendly, **or** he could be miserable.

* It was a warm day, **yet** storm clouds gathered over the distant mountains.

* It was a beautiful morning for a walk, **so** they set off quite happily.

2A - two adjectives

A *2A* sentence has two adjectives before the first noun, followed by two more adjectives before a second noun. This type of sentence is useful for creating a strong visual image in the reader's mind.

Examples

He was a tall, awkward man with an old, crumpled jacket.

    adj 1   adj 2   1st noun   adj 3   adj 4   2nd noun

It was an overgrown, messy garden with a lifeless, leafless tree.

    adj 1   adj 2 1st noun   adj 3   adj4 2nd noun

SIMILE - 'like a' / 'as a'

A simile sentence has a simile in the middle, which creates a vivid picture in the reader's mind. These are called 'like a' and 'as a' sentences to help you remember the comparison words you need to create similes.

Examples

The moon hung above us **like a** patient, pale, white face.

Although it was August, it was as cold **as a** late December evening.

3____ed – three related adjectives

A *3____ed* sentence begins with three related words, each of which ends in –ed. All the words must be followed by commas.

Examples

Frightened, terrified, exhausted, they ran from the creature.

Amused, amazed, excited, he left the circus reluctantly.

Confused, troubled, worried, she didn't know what had happened.

Most –ed words for this sentence type describe emotions.
Here are some –ed words for writing about a character's emotions.

A	appalled, angered	**M**	maddened, mellowed
B	bemused, bewildered	**N**	numbed, nurtured
C	confused, controlled	**O**	overawed, overjoyed
D	disappointed, dejected	**P**	perplexed, perturbed
E	excited, elated	**Q**	quietened, questioned
F	frightened, feared	**R**	relaxed, relieved
G	gladdened, guarded	**S**	shocked, startled
H	horrified, hated	**T**	terrified, troubled
I	interested, introverted	**U**	unnerved, uninterested
J	jaded, jinxed	**V**	vexed, valued
K	kind-hearted, knackered	**W**	worried, wretched
L	loved, loathed	**Z**	zonked, zapped

2 pairs

A *2 pairs* sentence begins with two pairs of related adjectives. Each pair is:

✱ followed by a comma

✱ separated by the conjunction 'and'.

Examples

Exhausted and worried, cold and hungry, they did not know how much further they had to go.

Injured and terrified, shell-shocked and lost, he wandered aimlessly across the battlefield.

Angry and bewildered, numb and fearful, she couldn't believe that this was happening to her.

De:De – description and details

A *De:De* sentence is a compound sentence, with two independent clauses separated by a colon. The first clause is descriptive and the second adds further detail. Using a colon shows that the information in the second clause will expand on the first part of the sentence.

Examples

The vampire is a dreadful creature: it kills by sucking all the blood from its victims.

Snails are slow: they take hours to cross the shortest of distances.

I was exhausted: I hadn't slept for more than two days.

Verb, person

It is possible to start a sentence with a verb in order to give greater importance to that verb. The verb should always be followed with a comma and then the name of a person (or a personal pronoun such as 'he', 'she', 'they' or 'it') and then the rest of the sentence.

Examples

Flinching, Kera turned quickly as the door slammed shut.

Crying, Julia ran towards her mother with a bleeding knee.

Hiding, Uzman breathed as quietly as he could.

Arguing, Alice and Zeba could be heard clearly by their neighbours.

O (I) - outside (inside)

O (I) sentences stands for 'outside (inside) sentences'. The first sentence tells the reader what a character is supposedly thinking. This is what is happening on the **outside**: the character's outward actions. The second sentence, which is always placed in brackets, lets the reader know the character's true **inner** feelings.

Examples

✳ He laughed heartily at the joke he had just been told. (At the same time it would be true to say he was quite embarrassed.)

✳ She told the little girl not to be so naughty. (Inside, however, she was secretly amused by what the little girl had done.)

✳ Mo said how pleased he was to be at the party. (It wasn't the truth - he longed to be elsewhere.)

If, if, if, then

If, if, if, then sentences have three dependent clauses in a series. They are often used:

* in speeches
* as a good opening to a story
* as a way to sum up a story.

Examples

If we buy less, **if** we recycle more, **if** we change our habits, **then** we can change the world.

If I was just a little taller, **if** I was just a little stronger, **if** I was just a little smarter, **then** I'd have a chance of beating my sister.

If I hadn't found that watch, **if** the alarm hadn't gone off, **if** it hadn't scared those burglars, **then** I wouldn't be sitting here today.

Emotion word, comma

These sentences start with an adjective describing an emotion, followed by a comma. The rest of the sentence describes actions which are related to the opening adjective. Placing the emotive adjective at the start of the sentence gives more importance to the emotion.

Examples

* Desperate, she screamed for help.

* Terrified, he froze instantly on the spot where he stood.

* Anxious, they began to realise that they were lost in the forest.

Noun: which / who / where

This sentence contains an embedded clause: an embedded clause can be removed and the sentence would still make sense without it. The sentence begins with a noun, followed by an embedded clause, which starts and ends with a comma. The final part of the sentence gives some detail.

Examples

Snakes, which scare me, are not always poisonous.

My bicycle, which is covered in mud, needs cleaning with warm soap and water.

Cakes, which taste fantastic, are not so good for your health.

Ad, same ad

An *Ad, same ad* sentence contains two identical adjectives, one repeated shortly after the other. The first is used in the opening clause of a sentence and the second is used immediately after the comma. Repeating adjectives like this can make them stick in the reader's mind.

Examples

He was a **smart** dresser, **smart** because he had the money to buy the best.

It was a **foolish** animal, **foolish** in a way that will become obvious as this story unfolds.

It was a **silent** town, **silent** in a way that did not make you feel restful.

She was a **fast** runner, **fast** because she needed to be.

3 bad (dash) question

A *3 bad (dash)* question begins with three negative words (adjectives or nouns). The third negative word is followed with a dash, then a question. By using three negatives, we can include a large amount of information in a short, dramatic sentence.

Examples

Greed, jealousy, hatred - which of these was Matei's worst trait?

Selfish, rude, unkind - how could Julia be any more obnoxious?

Thirst, heatstroke, exhaustion - which would kill him first?

Double -ly ending

A *Double -ly ending* sentence ends with two adverbs of manner. The first part of this sentence type ends in a verb, such as:

✱ *The worried people ran.*

This simple sentence is then extended by describing how the people ran:

✱ *The worried people ran quickly and purposefully.*

Examples

He swam slow**ly** and faltering**ly**.

She rode determined**ly** and swift**ly**.

He laughed loud**ly** and hearti**ly**.

All the Ws

All the Ws sentences are short sentences which begin with one of the following:

Who? What? When? Where? Why? Would? Was? Will? What if?

They are used:
* to directly involve the reader
* as an opening to a paragraph
* to arouse interest
* as an ending to invite the reader to decide.

Examples

Why do you think he ran away?

What next?

Why is our climate changing?

Will that really be the end?

List

This sentence is the simplest sentence form included in this book. It has no less than three and no more than four adjectives before a noun. It can create a striking visual impression in the reader's mind. Using alliteration can make the sentence even more dramatic.

Examples

* It was a dark, long, leafy lane.

* She had a cold, cruel cackle.

* It was a cold, wet, miserable and misty morning.

Some; others

Some; others sentences are compound sentences which begin with the word 'some' and end with the word 'other'. These sentences have two parts, separated by a semi-colon. They are useful for introducing a dilemma or an argument. They can also be a good way to start a story.

Examples

Some people love football; others just can't stand it.

Some days are full of enjoyment; others begin and end terribly.

Personification of weather

These sentences (also known as 'pathetic fallacy sentences') describe the weather as if it were a person. They are particularly useful for creating mood in a story. If you describe the rain as 'weeping', for example, it creates a sad mood.

Examples

* The wind screamed through the branches. (tense mood)

* The rain wept down the window. (sad mood)

* The breeze murmured through the branches. (happy mood)

* The snow smothered the town. (tense, claustrophobic mood)

The more, the more

The more, the more sentences use a paired form and are particularly useful when developing a character trait in a story. The first 'more' should be followed by an emotive word and the second 'more' should be followed by a related action.

Examples

The more upset she was, the more her tears flowed.

The more excited she became, the more talkative she seemed to be.

The more confused he became, the more he hammered his fist on the table.

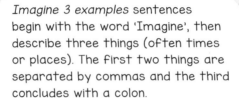
Imagine 3 examples

Imagine 3 examples sentences begin with the word 'Imagine', then describe three things (often times or places). The first two things are separated by commas and the third concludes with a colon.

The writer then explains that such a time or place exists. This is a superb sentence type to use at the start of a science fiction or fantasy story.

Examples

- Imagine a time <u>when people were not afraid</u>, <u>when life was much simpler</u>, <u>when everyone helped each other</u>: this is the story of that time.

- Imagine a place <u>where the sun always shines</u>, <u>where wars never happen</u>, <u>where no one ever dies</u>: in the Andromeda 5 system, there is such a planet.

3 Awesome alternatives

COLOURS

Red candy, cherry, crimson, rose, ruby, scarlet

Green basil, emerald, fern, moss, peridot, seaweed

Blue azure, cobalt, navy, royal, sapphire, true

Orange carrot, marigold, marmalade, fire, tiger

Yellow banana, butter, corn, honeybee, mustard, pineapple

Purple jam, lilac, magenta, plum, wine

NINJA TIP:

Use these alternatives with simple colour words like this, 'the **crimson** red coat', or on their own like this, 'an **emerald** leaf'.

COLOURS

Black

coal

ebony

jade

obsidian

soot

Brown

caramel

chocolate

coffee

gingerbread

mocha

walnut

Gold

blonde

butter

canary

daffodil

honey

medallion

Grey

ash

charcoal

fog

pewter

slate

smoke

Pink

blush

coral

flamingo

rose

strawberry

watermelon

White

bone

ivory

lace

pearl

rice

salt

NINJA TIP:

Use these alternatives with simple colour words like this, 'the **gingerbread** brown tree', or on their own like this, 'her **ivory** face'.

ALTERNATIVES: A–B

aggressive
combative, hostile, offensive, quarrelsome, warlike

amazing
breath-taking, fantastic, incredible, remarkable, splendid, staggering

angry
annoyed, cross, exasperated, fuming, irate, irritated

awesome
astonishing, exceptional, glorious, phenomenal, sensational

awful
dreadful, foul, ghastly, hideous, revolting, vile

bad
awful, dreadful, loathsome, rotten, wretched, vile

beautiful
angelic, appealing, bewitching, elegant, enticing, ravishing

big
gargantuan, immense, large, oversized, mammoth, vast

boring
dreary, dull, monotonous, repetitive, tedious, wearisome

brave
courageous, daring, gallant gutsy, heroic, intrepid

break
crack, fracture, obliterate, shatter, smash, wreck

bright
blazing, brilliant, clear, incandescent, light, luminous

ALTERNATIVES: C

* **calm**
  peaceful, quiet, serene, still, undisturbed, tranquil

* **cold**
  biting, bitter, chilly, freezing, sub-zero

* **colourful**
  radiant, rainbow, rich, multicoloured, psychedelic, vivid

* **come**
  advance, approach, arrive, join, near, reach

* **confused**
  disorientated, perplexed, puzzled, sketchy, unclear, woolly

* **cry**
  bawl, scream, sob, weep, whimper, yowl

* **curly**
  crinkly, frizzy, kinked, ringleted, wavy, wiry

* **cute**
  attractive, charming, delightful, enchanting, lovely, sweet

ALTERNATIVES: D-E

dangerous
hazardous, murderous, savage, threatening, vicious

dark
dim, dusky, gloomy, murky, shaded, sunless

dead
fallen, lifeless, lost, perished, slain, slaughtered

destroy
annihilate, damage, impair, ravage, shatter, wreck

different
clashing, conflicting, contrasting, contradictory, opposed, unlike

difficult
back-breaking, challenging, demanding, exhausting, strenuous, taxing

drink
consume, chug, sip, swallow, swig, swill

easy
effortless, elementary, simple, painless, straightforward, uncomplicated

eat
chew, consume, demolish, devour, munch, swallow

enjoy
adore, fancy, like, love, relish, savour

epic
impressive, remarkable, sweet, thrilling, unforgettable

excited
aroused, eager, ecstatic, enthusiastic, perky, roused

ALTERNATIVES: F-G

✑ **faint** ....light, muted, stifled, subdued, thin, weak

✑ **fall** ....dive, nosedive, plummet, plunge, trip, tumble

✑ **famous** ....eminent, infamous, leading, legendary, popular, well-known

✑ **fast** ....blistering, breakneck, nimble, quick, rapid, speedy

✑ **fat** ....chubby, overweight, plump, rotund, solid, stout

✑ **find** ....detect, discover, learn, notice, observe, realise

✑ **finish** ....cease, complete, conclude, end, fulfil, terminate

✑ **food** ....cuisine, fodder, grub, meal, nourishment, supplies

✑ **fly** ....float, flutter, glide, hang, hover, soar

✑ **frightened** ....alarmed, fearful, panicked, petrified, spooked, startled

✑ **fun** ....amusing, entertaining, enthralling, exciting, lively, pleasing

✑ **ginormous** ....colossal, monumental, sizeable, tremendous, vast, whopping

✑ **go** ....continue, leave, move, proceed, travel, visit

✑ **good** ....excellent, exceptional, marvellous, splendid, stupendous, super

ALTERNATIVES: H

happy
delighted, ecstatic, glad, joyous, overjoyed, thrilled

hate
despise, detest, dislike, execrate, fear, loathe

have
boast, keep, occupy, own, possess, retain

hello
greetings, hey, hi, howdy, morning, welcome

help
advise, aid, assist, contribute, guide, support

hide
cache, camouflage, conceal, obstruct, shroud, stow

high
elevated, lofty, sky-scraping, soaring, tall, towering

hold
carry, cradle, embrace, grasp, grip, squeeze

hot
blistering, roasting, scorching, summery, tropical

hungry
malnourished, peckish, ravenous, starved, starving, underfed

hurt
damage, incapacitate, injure, maim, mutilate, wound

kick
blast, boot, punt, send, smash, welly

kill
decimate, destroy, eliminate, exterminate, massacre, slay

kind
altruistic, caring, compassionate, gentle, unselfish, warm

large
colossal, cumbersome, huge, immense, monstrous, vast

lazy
idle, inactive, lethargic, slothful, sluggish, workshy

like
akin, alike, equivalent, related, similar, twin

little
compact, delicate, minor, small, teeny, tiny

long
lengthy, longer, extended, extensive, prolonged, protracted

look
gawp, glance, examine, inspect, peer, stare

loud
blasting, booming, deafening, ear-piercing, thunderous

love
adore, cherish, idolise, prize, treasure, worship

lovely
adorable, appealing, attractive, beautiful, exquisite, magical

ALTERNATIVES: M-N

- **make**
assemble, cause, concoct, create, fabricate, produce

- **many**
abundance, countless, numerous, multiple, shedload

- **massive**
enormous, herculean, huge, monstrous, towering, vast

- **messy**
bombsite, chaotic, dirty, disorderly, scruffy, untidy

- **move**
carry, relocate, shift, transfer, transport

- **moved**
ambled, crept, dashed, lurked, maneuvered, shuffled

- **mysterious**
baffling, curious, funny, inexplicable, puzzling, strange

- **nervous**
anxious, hysterical, jumpy, neurotic, tense, timid

- **new**
contemporary, current, fresh, modern, pristine, unused

- **nice**
admirable, congenial, enjoyable, likeable, lovely, thoughtful

- **noise**
commotion, din, hubbub, pandemonium, sound, uproar

ALTERNATIVES: O-Q

✲ old
ancient, elderly, frayed,
historic, mature, tattered

✲ pick
appoint, assign, choose,
designate, identify, select

✲ ok
acceptable, average, decent,
fair, fine, satisfactory

✲ play
cavort, compete, engage,
frolic, interact, romp

ALTERNATIVES: R-S

really actually, certainly, genuinely, truly, undoubtedly,
unquestionably

rich affluent, flush, loaded, minted, wealthy, well-off

run dash, hurtle, rush, scamper, scurry, scuttle

sad blue, depressed, desolate, down, glum, unhappy

☆ poor
bad, crummy, diabolical, faulty, rotten, shoddy

✴ pretty
appealing, charming, delightful, glamorous, lovely, stunning

☆ put
deposit, lay, place, plonk, position, set

✴ quickly
briskly, hotfoot, lickety-split, rapidly, speedily, swiftly

☆ quiet
calming, restful, serene, soundless, still, tranquil

said	acknowledged, insisted, laughed, reported, stammered, thundered
scared	afraid, agitated, alarmed, fearful, nervous, panicky
scary	blood-curdling, daunting, formidable, frightened, hair-raising, spine-chilling
sick	diseased, ill, nauseous, poorly, unhealthy, unwell
shout	bellow, call, cry, howl, shriek, yell
sleep	catnap, doze, drowse, rest, siesta

slow
creep, dawdling, gentle, leisurely, plod, sluggish

small
bijou, little, microscopic, mini, minute, tiny

soft
flexible, malleable, silky, spongy, springy, supple

stop
cease, conclude, end, finish, suspend, terminate

strong
meaty, mighty, muscular, powerful, robust, strapping

stuff
gear, goods, items, objects, possessions, property

stupid
dense, dim, dumb, foolish, ignorant, imbecile

suddenly
abruptly, immediately, instantaneously, instantly, promptly, swiftly

sunny
balmy, bright, clear, fair, fine, summery

ALTERNATIVES: T-V

- **take**
capture, grab, pilfer, remove, seize, steal

- **talk**
blabber, chat, converse, gossip, natter, speak

- **tell**
advise, alert, declare, inform, notify, warn

- **terrible**
appalling, atrocious, awful, dreadful, revolting

- **then**
after, afterwards, instantly, later, next, soon, subsequently

- **think**
deliberate, meditate, muse, ponder, reflect, ruminate

- **thought**
considered, contemplated, mused, pondered, reasoned

- **tired**
drained, drowsy, exhausted, jaded, shattered, weary

- **ugly**
deformed, grotesque, hideous, menacing, plain, unsightly

- **unhappy**
despondent, dispirited, down, forlorn, miserable

- **very**
exceedingly, desperately, hugely, immensely, mightily, overly

ALTERNATIVES: W-Y

wait
delay, linger, loiter, remain, rest, stay

walk
amble, plod, roam, stroll, wander

weak
delicate, feeble, flimsy, fragile, frail, powerless

weird
bizarre, eerie, peculiar, surreal, uncanny, unconventional

went
departed, journeyed, moved, proceeded, progressed, travelled

wet
damp, drenched, moist, saturated, soaked, waterlogged

wild
blustering, howling, nasty, raging, stormy, windy

win
achieve, acquire, gain, obtain, scoop, secure

young
adolescent, babyish, childlike, immature, juvenile, youthful

4 Alternative verb choices

(INFERENCE-RICH VERBS)

SAID: SPEECH VERBS

The most common word we use in writing when someone is speaking is, 'said'. However, there are lots of other words we can use to show *how* someone is speaking.

Loud

- bellowed
- echoed
- screamed
- shouted
- yelled

Quiet

- hesitated
- mumbled
- murmured
- whispered

SAID: SPEECH VERBS
(continued)

Conversation
- answered
- argued
- blurted
- replied

Funny
- cackled
- chortled
- chuckled
- giggled
- sniggered

Angry
- growled
- pestered
- ranted
- roared
- scolded

Sad
- cried
- moaned
- wept
- whimpered
- whined

Happy
- boasted
- bragged
- crowed
- exclaimed
- purred

Tired
- panted
- sighed
- yawned

GET AND GOT

Moving in and out

For example, rather than saying, 'I got out', you could say, 'I stumbled out'.

amble / ambled

bounce / bounced

bumble / bumbled

crawl / crawled

creep / crept

dance / danced

dawdle / dawdled

dive / dived

escape / escaped

exit / exited

flip / flipped

gallop / galloped

head / headed

hop / hopped

idle / idled

jump / jumped

leap / leapt

mope / moped

move / moved

nip / nipped

prance / pranced

race / raced

roll / rolled

slither / slithered

step / stepped

stumble / stumbled

tip-toe / tip-toed

tumble / tumbled

walk / walked

wander / wandered

wobble / wobbled

zoom / zoomed

GET AND GOT

Receiving or requiring

For example, instead of 'I got a pizza',
you could say 'I ordered a pizza'.

- accept / accepted
- acquire / acquired
- arrive / arrived
- buy / bought
- catch / caught
- collect / collected
- control / controlled
- discover / discovered
- fight / fought
- find / found
- gather / gathered

- locate / located
- obtain / obtained
- order / ordered
- pick up / picked up
- pinch / pinched
- purchase / purchased
- receive / received
- secure / secured
- steal / stole
- uncover / uncovered
- withdraw / withdrew

GO AND WENT

Here are some alternative words to describe travelling or moving. For example, rather than saying, 'she went', you could say, 'she pranced'.

ambled / ambled
bike / biked
climb / climbed
cycle / cycled
drive / drove
elope / eloped
float / floated
fly / flew
glide / glided

hike / hiked
hop / hopped
idle / idled
jump / jumped
kayak / kayaked
limp / limped
meander / meandered
move / moved
navigate / navigated
oscillate / oscillated
prance / pranced
run / ran
sail / sailed
sashay / sashayed
sneak / sneaked
sprint / sprinted
travel / travelled
visit / visited
walk / walked
wander / wandered

WANT AND WANTED

Here are some alternative words to say something is wanted or needed. For example, rather than saying, 'I want a new book', you could say, 'I desire a new book'.

crave / craved

desire / desired

fancy / fancied

hope for / hoped for

need / needed

require / required

wish for / wished for

would like

5 Setting vocabulary

SETTING VOCABULARY TIPS

When describing a setting, think about the following things and try to describe them in a complete sentence or more.

* Describe the setting in the distance - show, don't tell. (Show far)

* Describe the setting that is near. Focus on one thing in detail that catches the eye but don't use its name. (Show near)

* Describe the colours, shapes and movements of objects. (Show colours and objects)

* What can you hear? Where is it coming from? Is it loud or quiet? (Show sounds)

* Are there any smells or tastes that you can describe? (Show senses)

* Describe something that's moving and use personification. (Show using personification)

* Compare the setting to something normal and familiar like a busy city centre. (Show comparative setting)

* Describe something that changes like the light, sounds or temperature. (Show a change)

* How does this change affect the mood and atmosphere? (Show mood change)

* Finally, explain where you actually are and how the character may feel. (Tell)

SPRING / SUMMER

Adjectives

- bright
- cloudless
- fragrant
- humid
- leisurely
- moist
- refreshing
- scorching
- shaded
- sizzling
- sunburnt
- sun-kissed
- sweating
- unforgettable

Nouns

- adventure
- barbecue
- blossom
- campfire
- dandelion
- heatwave
- humidity
- iced water
- picnic
- rain shower
- sandcastle
- temperature
- tourist
- weather

Verbs

- camp
- celebrate
- cool down
- build
- exercise
- float
- frolic
- grill
- perspire
- quench
- relax
- sweat
- swim
- uncover

AUTUMN / WINTER

Adjectives

blustery
colourful
crunchy
enchanting
foraging
frostbitten
glistening
insulated
leafless
nippy
powdery
shivering
slippery
wintery

Nouns

bonfire
cobwebs
cough
foliage
frost
hail
harvest
insulation
mittens
scarecrow
shovel
snowball
snowstorm
whiteout

Verbs

build
clear
freeze
glare
glisten
hibernate
jungle
melt
shiver
ski
sled
sneeze
snuggle
wrap

WOODLAND / FOREST

Adjectives

blossoming
breathtaking
darkened
dense
fast-growing
fragrant
gloomy
impenetrable
luscious
multicoloured
shadowy
stunning
sun-kissed
vast

Nouns

branch
canopy
habitat
insect
leaves
logs
moss
shadow
soil
stream
thicket
timber
vegetation
vines

Verbs

brush
build
chop
clear
climb
discover
enter
explore
hang
investigate
listen
sneak
sway
traverse

CITY / TOWN

Adjectives

- ✷ bustling
- ✷ busy
- ✷ congested
- ✷ dangerous
- ✷ flourishing
- ✷ inner
- ✷ modern
- ✷ neon
- ✷ noisy
- ✷ overcrowded
- ✷ picturesque
- ✷ polluted
- ✷ smoky
- ✷ unknown

Nouns

- ✷ cafe
- ✷ hospital
- ✷ hotel
- ✷ motorway
- ✷ police
- ✷ public
- ✷ restaurant
- ✷ skyscraper
- ✷ station
- ✷ streetlights
- ✷ supermarket
- ✷ train
- ✷ transport
- ✷ underground

Verbs

- ✷ buy
- ✷ communicate
- ✷ commute
- ✷ cycle
- ✷ dine
- ✷ employ
- ✷ inhabit
- ✷ rent
- ✷ sleep
- ✷ socialise
- ✷ travel
- ✷ visit
- ✷ walk
- ✷ work

DAY / NIGHT / EVENING

Adjectives	Nouns	Verbs
beautiful	afternoon	approach
chilly	breakfast	cast
colourful	clouds	cool
dark	dawn	cover
early	dusk	float
eerie	evening	hide
fresh	lunchtime	hover
late	midday	remember
light	midnight	reveal
memorable	moonlight	rise
mild	morning	see
soundless	shadow	set
unforgettable	sunset	shine
warm	sunshine	warm

SPOOKY / HAUNTED

Adjectives	Nouns	Verbs
abandoned	atmosphere	break
chilling	bats and birds	escape
creepy	building	explore
dilapidated	darkness	flee
enticing	door handle	haunt
forgotten	figure	hide
frightening	floorboard	investigate
ghostly	ghost	peer
haunting	gravestone	possess
murky	graveyard	pursue
mysterious	senses	reveal
sinister	shadow	scream
spooky	spectre	sneak
translucent	spirit	whisper

OCEAN / COAST / RIVER

Adjectives
- beautiful
- blustery
- delicious
- enormous
- natural
- picturesque
- refreshing
- roaring
- rolling
- sandy
- sparkling
- sprawling
- sumptuous
- towering

Nouns
- beach
- bucket and spade
- crab
- dam
- dune
- fish and chips
- fishing
- ice cream
- ocean
- rock pool
- seabird
- sea fret
- stream
- waterfall

Verbs
- breathe
- build
- buy
- climb
- crash
- dip
- float
- frolic
- inhale
- sail
- search
- stroll
- taste
- visit

SCHOOL

Adjectives	Nouns	Verbs
broken	assembly	bully
caring	breaktime	celebrate
creative	caretaker	clean
disruptive	classroom	compete
helpful	cloakroom	embarrass
intelligent	detention	expel
interesting	hall	experiment
naughty	headteacher	fight
perfect	office	learn
powerful	PE cupboard	register
respectful	playground	reward
unknown	pupils	separate
unruly	staffroom	shout
worrying	teacher	teach

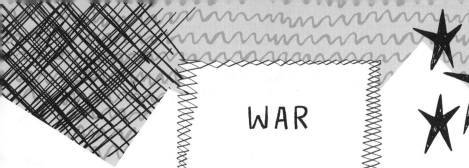

WAR

Adjectives	Nouns	Verbs
battered	ammunition	assault
deadly	barbed wire	capture
explosive	battlefield	dent
horrific	bayonet	destroy
horrifying	enemy	entangle
innocent	helmet	evacuate
lifesaving	mortar shell	excavate
military	prisoner	explode
nightmarish	remembrance	imprison
sickening	rifle	protect
sinister	soldier	release
unforgettable	tank	retreat
unforgiving	trench	save
unpleasant	uniform	trap

SPACE

Adjectives

brave
cosmic
dangerous
enormous
mysterious
reflective
rugged
scorching
sparkling
unexplained
unexplored
unknown
vast
vital

Nouns

alien
asteroid
astronaut
atmosphere
earth
gravity
meteor
moon
oxygen
planet
solar system
shuttle
sun
universe

Verbs

crash
discover
explore
fall
float
invade
launch
manoeuvre
orbit
plummet
radio
research
rotate
travel

CHARACTER VOCAB

GENERAL VOCAB

MY NOTES

PIRATE / ADVENTURE

Adjectives	Nouns	Verbs
backstabbing	adventurer	clash
bountiful	cannon	deal
brave	captain	deceive
dangerous	compass	bury
deadly	doctor	explore
devious	first mate	fight
huge	flag	follow
infamous	hull	sail
lost	mast	salute
nasty	pirate	shipwreck
strong	sail	shout
swashbuckling	sailor	strand
unsavoury	treasure	trick
valuable	treasure map	wave

HOME

SETTING VOCAB

CHARACTER VOCAB

GENERAL VOCAB

MY NOTES

Adjectives

* aromatic
* clean
* comfy
* dirty
* disgusting
* disorganised
* familiar
* greasy
* homely
* luxurious
* messy
* organised
* pristine
* well-used

Nouns

* attic / loft
* bathroom
* bedroom
* cellar
* conservatory
* dining room
* driveway
* flat
* garage
* garden
* kitchen
* living room
* shed
* stairs

Verbs

* break
* clean
* cook
* cut
* fix
* install
* live
* prune
* remove
* repair
* sleep
* stack
* store
* wash

69

SETTLEMENT

Adjectives

ancient
brave
clever
essential
exhausting
fearsome
heavy
naive
natural
old
primitive
sharp
thick
vulnerable

Nouns

animal
campfire
clay
crops
field
hunter
hut
instrument
leader
mud
pelt
straw
tool
well

Verbs

collect
cook
crush
cultivate
explore
farm
forage
grow
harvest
hunt
invade
knit
nurture
rear

SPORTS

Adjectives	Nouns	Verbs
brave	attacker	argue
crammed	captain	celebrate
determined	defender	cheer
dirty	manager	cross
fair	opposition	lift
fast	players	pass
glittering	referee	roar
intelligent	spectator	score
hard-working	stadium	select
lazy	substitute	shoot
spirited	team	shout
strong	teammate	substitute
sweaty	tracksuit	swap
united	trophy	tackle

MYSTERY / SUSPENSE

Adjectives

- deadly
- devious
- elusive
- innocent
- intelligent
- mysterious
- scary
- secret
- secretive
- super
- suspicious
- unforeseen
- unusual
- various

Nouns

- accident
- clues
- detective
- magnifying glass
- map
- murder
- mystery
- plan
- secret
- sidekick
- suspect
- victim
- villain
- weapon

Verbs

- accuse
- alert
- collaborate
- collect
- commit
- deceive
- discover
- erupt
- identify
- plot
- predict
- remove
- suspect
- understand

GAMING / IMAGINARY

Adjectives	Nouns	Verbs
brave	adventure	attack
camouflaged	avatar	buffer
colourful	boss	build
dangerous	character	buy / purchase
enchanted	enemy	cheat
evil	equipment	complete
imaginary	level	create
infamous	hack	defend
invisible	magic	discover
luminous	outfit	evolve
magical	sidekick	lag
powerful	skill	navigate
skilful	skin	race
special	world	transport

FOREIGN COUNTRY

Adjectives

ancient
beautiful
cultured
exciting
famous
historic
magnificent
picturesque
tropical
unique
vast
vibrant
war-torn
well-known

Nouns

airport
architecture
buildings
capital city
cuisine
culture
flag
holiday
language
souvenir
statue
tour
tourist
transport

Verbs

absorb
create
experience
explore
fly
learn
leave
observe
photograph
share
talk
tour
travel
visit

FAIRYTALE / CASTLE

Adjectives	Nouns	Verbs
brave	curse	battle
charming	damsel	climb
clever	goblin	curse
evil	hero	die
fair	knight	dream
gallant	maiden	fall
gentle	ogre	fight
graceful	palace	kill
grumpy	prince	kiss
handsome	princess	love
helpful	quest	poison
mean	tower	rescue
scary	witch	search
wise	wizard	transform

MYTHS AND LEGENDS

Adjectives	Nouns	Verbs
beautiful	beast	behead
brave	dragon	breathe fire
coarse	enemy	charge
cryptic	field	chop
cunning	hero	destroy
disgusting	labyrinth	devour
enormous	map	fly
hairy	monster	hiss
hideous	potion	investigate
hypnotic	river	puncture
impenetrable	shield	sail
poisonous	temple	scream
scaly	underworld	soar
sneaky	weapon	stir

6 Character vocabulary

CHARACTER VOCABULARY TIPS

When describing a character, think about the following things and try to describe them in a complete sentence or more.

* Describe what they are wearing, giving the names, colours and the condition of their clothing.

* Describe their height and build.

* Describe their eyes and hair. You could use a simile to describe their eye and hair colour.

* Describe the character's facial features in detail, for example, a scar, crooked nose, or a flash of white hair.

* Use personification to create a mental image of the character's clothing.

* Describe how this character makes other people feel.

* Describe the equipment the character has with them.

* Say how the weather is affecting the character's appearance.

* Use an oxymoron to compare or contrast the character. An oxymoron is when two opposite words are used, such as 'a deafening silence'.

HAIR

Adjectives	Nouns	Verbs
❀ ageing	✳ bobble	❀ cover
✳ bald	❀ bun	✳ curl
❀ blonde	✳ clippers	❀ dry
✳ colourful	❀ curls	✳ fall
❀ curly	✳ follicle	❀ grow
✳ dark	❀ fringe	✳ hang
❀ frizzy	✳ hair band	❀ hide
✳ golden	❀ hair clip	✳ rest
❀ luscious	✳ patch	❀ roll
✳ pale	❀ plait	✳ smooth
❀ straight	✳ ponytail	❀ stand
✳ thick	❀ sideburn	✳ straighten
❀ wavy	✳ strand	❀ toss
✳ wild	❀ style	✳ wrap

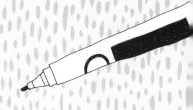

FACE

Adjectives

- ageing
- appealing
- battered
- dry
- glowing
- neat
- noticeable
- pale
- radiant
- scared
- smooth
- tanned
- tired
- youthful

Nouns

- beard
- cheek
- chin
- ears
- eye
- eyebrow
- eyelid
- forehead
- lips
- mole
- mouth
- moustache
- nose
- wrinkle

Verbs

- blink
- close
- flicker
- frown
- grimace
- grow
- itch
- open
- rise
- shudder
- sneeze
- twitch
- widen
- wrinkle

EYES

Adjectives	Nouns	Verbs
beautiful	cheek	blink
colourful	contact lens	hide
deep	cornea	inspect
delicate	eyebrow	ogle
iridescent	eyelashes	peer
long	eyelid	protect
luscious	forehead	rest
metallic	glasses	shade
protective	goggles	shadow
reflective	iris	spy
sparkling	make-up	stare
translucent	mascara	twitch
watery	pupil	view
unforgettable	sunglasses	wink

NOSE

Adjectives

broken
bulging
busted
crooked
dainty
gruesome
gunky
hairy
long
perfect
pointy
slim
symmetrical
undulating

Nouns

blemish
bogey
bridge
finger
fluid
freckles
hair
handkerchief
nostril
skin
snot
snout
spot
tissue

Verbs

blow
breathe
cover
eject
inhale
pick
smell
sneeze
sniff
sniffle
snort
tickle
wiggle
wipe

SKIN

Adjectives	Nouns	Verbs
ageing	cell	burn
ancient	colour	clean
burnt	complexion	cover
cracked	condition	cut
dark	crease	damage
experienced	fold	decorate
light	freckle	heal
old	hair	moisturise
olive	layer	paint
scared	mole	protect
soft	organ	repair
tattooed	story	scrape
young	tattoo	scrub
youthful	wrinkle	wash

ARMS AND LEGS

Adjectives

- bony
- brittle
- broad
- broken
- clenched
- crooked
- damaged
- infected
- narrow
- perfect
- powerful
- scarred
- strong
- weak

Nouns

- ankle
- biceps
- calf
- elbow
- finger
- fingernail
- fist
- forearm
- heel
- knee
- palm
- shin
- shoulders
- toenail

Verbs

- bash
- break
- clench
- clip
- cut
- extend
- flex
- injure
- itch
- knock
- rub
- smash
- stroke
- wave

BODY

Adjectives	Nouns	Verbs
broad	back	beat
chiselled	blood	bounce
feeble	bones	deliver
huge	bottom	explore
mishapen	chest	flow
muscular	chin	grow
pale	face	hang
pointy	hair	open
powerful	head	protect
rich	heart	protrude
round	lungs	pulse
scarred	muscles	relax
soft	saliva	scratch
weak	skin	work

CLOTHING / APPEARANCE

Adjectives

* brand-new
* bullet-holed
* camouflaged
* functional
* muddy
* pristine
* protective
* second-hand
* stylish
* tarnished
* tired
* torn
* warm
* waterproof

Nouns

* balaclava
* boots
* cape
* coat
* dress
* gilet
* gloves
* hat
* hood
* jacket
* satchel
* scarf
* skirt
* snood

Verbs

* attract
* cover
* feel
* fit
* flap
* fly
* hang
* hide
* hug
* protect
* restrict
* shield
* wave
* wrap

HEIGHT / BUILD

Adjectives	Nouns	Verbs
broad	arms	block
chunky	aura	bulge
large	back	destroy
miniature	body	excite
rotund	chest	hang
short	face	infuriate
similar	feet	inspire
stumpy	fingers	intimidate
tall	head	protect
thick	height	protrude
thin	legs	reveal
tiny	neck	scare
unusual	stomach	sicken
wide	waist	tower

VOICE

Adjectives	Nouns	Verbs
booming	argument	bellow
brittle	chat	cough
childlike	conversation	echo
deafening	dialogue	groan
gruff	discussion	howl
heated	joke	moan
high-pitched	natter	scream
hoarse	poem	shout
husky	quarrel	shriek
loud	reply	spew
muted	report	squeal
quiet	song	stutter
raucous	speech	talk
wheezy	tone	whisper

EQUIPMENT

Adjectives	Nouns	Verbs
beautiful	binoculars	call
dangerous	first aid kit	climb
intricate	flare	compute
latest	laser	enter
metal	map	hang
new	necklace	hold
plastic	phone	lasso
scuffed	rope	locate
stained	rucksack	pinpoint
state-of-the-art	spade	repair
sturdy	sunglasses	search
tarnished	tablet	store
torn	telescope	tunnel
versatile	utility belt	zoom in

QUIRKS

- always lies
- bites lip
- bites fingernails
- checks watch
- clenches fists
- clicks fingers
- clumsy
- coughs loudly
- cracks knuckles
- fiddles with ear lobe
- flares nostrils
- flutters eyelids
- foot tapping
- glances sideways
- grinds teeth
- hallucinates
- has invisible friend
- head bobbing
- head in hands
- head tilting

- heavy breathing
- ignores others
- looks down at feet
- looks in the mirror a lot
- mumbles things
- never sleeps
- nose twitching
- peers over glasses
- quivering chin
- raises eyebrows
- rolls eyes
- rubs neck
- scratches head
- shrugs shoulders
- snorts when laughing
- sweats profusely
- tosses hair
- twiddles thumbs
- walks back and forth
- washes hands constantly

PERSONALITY

Positive

affectionate
ambitious
brave
caring
cheerful
concerned

confident
considerate
curious
devoted
elegant
focused
honest

loyal
modest
patient
punctual
resilient
sincere
sympathetic

thoughtful
thrifty
trustworthy
warm
willing
worthy

Negative

- angry
- argumentative
- clumsy
- coarse
- complacent
- crafty
- cynical
- fickle

- flamboyant
- frivolous
- greedy
- gullible
- hateful
- impulsive
- moody
- narrow-minded
- nonchalant

- sarcastic
- shy
- silly
- sloppy
- stupid
- superficial
- timid
- violent
- weak

General vocabulary

GENERAL VOCABULARY TIPS

When choosing vocabulary, think about the following things to make your writing better, different or more engaging.

* Try to spot words that you are repeating often and see if you can change them. Instead of repeating names, can you use a pronoun instead such as, 'he', 'she', 'they', 'the boys' or 'the girls'?

* Pair adjectives together to add description, such as 'a **large**, **crumbling** building'.

* Start some sentences with fronted adverbials to show location, mood and time.

* When using a verb, try to use an adverb with it to give more detail.

* Use similar adjectives together to enhance your description, such as '**kind** and **caring**'.

* When you use a noun, add an adjective to describe it.

* Avoid using 'got', 'get' and 'went' a lot. Can you choose other verbs instead?

* Build phrases, which are groups of words, rather than just using single words.

* Use similes and metaphors with interesting vocabulary to create images in the reader's mind.

MY NOTES

SIMILES

Similes compare two objects by using 'like' and 'as'.
Similes are useful as they can help the reader
to create an image in their mind.

- Caio erupted like a volcano.

- Mia's hands trembled like the earth during an earthquake.

- Kind like a queen.

- Last night, I slept like a log.

- She was as brave as a lion.

- Sweat ran down his face like a waterfall.

- The audience listened to the speech as quietly as mice.

- The sheets were as soft as silk.

- The wind howled like a pack of wolves.

- They are as different as night and day.

- We were blind as bats and couldn't find our way out.

- He wobbled like a candle in the wind.

METAPHORS

Metaphors are used to compare two separate objects using 'is' and 'are'. They are useful as they can help the reader to create an image in their mind.

- Ben's temper was a volcano, ready to explode.
- Books are the keys to your imagination.
- He is a shining star.
- He is a walking dictionary.
- Her angry words were bullets to him.
- Her long hair was a flowing golden river.
- Her lovely voice was music to his ears.
- His tears were a river flowing down his cheeks.
- Her heart is a cold iron.
- Jamal was a pig at dinner.
- Kisses are the flowers of affection.
- Life is a rollercoaster.
- Maria is a chicken.
- Nur's eyes were fireflies.
- My big sister is a couch potato.
- My dad is a road hog.
- My kid's room is a disaster area.
- My teacher is a dragon.
- She is a beautiful peacock.

MY NOTES

MORE METAPHORS

- ⚚ Thank you so much; you are an angel.

- ✱ That lawn is a green carpet.

- ⚚ The alligator's teeth are white daggers.

- ✱ The ballerina was a swan, gliding across the stage.

- ⚚ The calm lake was a mirror.

- ✱ The car was a furnace in the sun.

- ⚚ The children were flowers grown in concrete gardens.

- ✱ The classroom was a zoo.

- ⚚ The clouds are balls of cotton.

- ✱ The falling snowflakes are dancers.

- ⚚ The kids were monkeys on the jungle gym.

- ✱ The lightning was fireworks in the sky.

- ⚚ The moon is a white balloon.

- ✱ The park was a lake after the rain.

* The road ahead was a ribbon stretching across the desert.

* The snow is a white blanket.

* The stars are sparkling diamonds.

* The stormy ocean was a raging bull.

* The sun is a golden ball.

* The teenager's stomach was a bottomless pit.

* The thunder was a mighty lion.

* The wind was a howling wolf.

* Their home was a prison.

* Those best friends are two peas in a pod.

* Tom's eyes were ice as he stared at her.

* Your brain is a computer.

MY NOTES

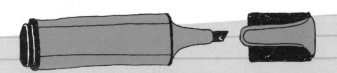

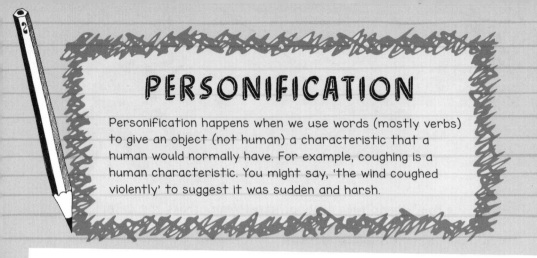

PERSONIFICATION

Personification happens when we use words (mostly verbs) to give an object (not human) a characteristic that a human would normally have. For example, coughing is a human characteristic. You might say, 'the wind coughed violently' to suggest it was sudden and harsh.

- The kettle whistled an angry tune as it came to the boil.

- The grease jumped out of the pan.

- The curtains danced in the breeze.

- The fruit dived from the branches of the trees, down towards the ground.

- Hailstones crashed into and thumped the ageing windows.

- The tree branch scratched and clawed at my windowsill, trying to break into the house.

- During the night, the blanket crept up until it was snuggled under my chin.

- Books stood on the library shelves like soldiers.

- The mother duck scolded her young, encouraging them to walk in a line.

- Rays from the sun danced down towards the earth.

- The diving board taunted me, daring me to approach.

- Waves gently tickled her toes while sand climbed up between her toes.

ANIMALS

Adjectives	Nouns	Verbs
deadly	antler	attack
desirable	beak	chase
flexible	claw	consume
impenetrable	fin	defend
imperfect	fur	disable
jagged	horn	hibernate
piercing	scales	howl
rough	shell	hunt
sharp	teeth	laze
slimy	tongue	preen
staggering	trunk	pursue
streamlined	venom	rest
thoughtful	vertebrae	stalk
unique	wings	swoop

PEOPLE

Adjectives	Nouns	Verbs
affectionate	aunt	buy
angry	brother	clean
annoying	carer	cook
caring	cousin	fix
distant	father	hug
emotional	friend	laugh
forgetful	gran	love
kind	grandad	order
lazy	half-brother	repair
loving	half-sister	shout
loyal	mother	sleep
strict	nan	tickle
	sibling	tidy
	sister	visit
	step-brother	
	step-sister	
	uncle	

TRANSPORT

Adjectives

agile
breakable
clean
cumbersome
dangerous
electronic
expensive
frequent
hefty
nimble
organised
reliable
slow
streamlined

Nouns

aeroplane
bicycle
bus
car
dustbin lorry
ferry
forklift truck
helicopter
lorry
motorbike
taxi
train
tram
van

Verbs

collect
control
crash
deliver
escort
fly
hover
indicate
learn
manoeuvre
overtake
pick up
ride
travel

MY NOTES

FOOD AND DRINK

Adjectives
- bitter
- burnt
- delicious
- disgusting
- edible
- foul
- frozen
- inedible
- memorable
- raw
- sour
- succulent
- sweet
- tasty
- yucky

Nouns
- breakfast
- chef
- cook
- dessert
- dinner
- ingredients
- kitchen
- lunch
- meal
- restaurant
- snack
- supper
- tea
- takeaway
- utensils

Verbs
- bite
- chew
- chop
- consume
- cook
- defrost
- fry
- guzzle
- inhale
- nibble
- prepare
- regurgitate
- scoff
- serve
- sip

CITIES

Adjectives

alluring
beautiful
busy
creative
cultured
different
European
historic
inspiring
interesting
memorable
narrow
unusual
vast

Nouns

Amsterdam
Athens
Beijing
Belfast
Berlin
Canberra
Cardiff
Dublin
Edinburgh
Lisbon
London
Madrid
New Dehli
Paris
Rome
Shanghai
Tokyo

Verbs

arrive
buy
eat
exhaust
experience
explore
leave
photograph
relax
remember
see
tour
video
visit

MY NOTES

TECHNOLOGY

Adjectives	Nouns	Verbs
addictive	app	block
clever	computer	code
dangerous	cyber bullying	create
digital	email	destroy
efficient	gaming	develop
electronic	gigabyte	google
enabling	internet	help
endless	media	post
enormous	message	request
evil	mobile phone	research
exciting	social media	search
helpful	tablet	share
productive	video call	
useful	video game	

JOBS

Adjectives	Nouns	Verbs
brave	actor	care
caring	architect	connect
clever	artist	defend
creative	builder	diagnose
dedicated	designer	entertain
experienced	doctor	fight
important	electrician	inspire
inspirational	musician	perform
knowledgeable	nurse	play
naive	plumber	protect
new	soldier	recite
selfless	sportsperson	repair
skilled	stylist	support
vital	teacher	teach

MY NOTES

POSITIVE EMOTIONS

- amused
- appreciated
- competent
- creative
- curious
- delighted
- empowered
- enthusiastic
- excited
- exhilarated
- grateful
- included
- interested
- loved
- passionate
- proud
- relaxed
- safe
- satisfied
- unique
- valued

NEGATIVE EMOTIONS

- abandoned
- alone
- betrayed
- bitter
- cheated
- claustrophobic
- confused
- disgusted
- embarrassed
- failed
- frustrated
- guilty
- lonely
- manipulated
- numb
- panicky
- shattered
- terrified
- tormented
- unwanted
- vulnerable

COLLECTIVE NOUNS

Collective nouns are used to name groups of things, especially animals.

A
a herd of **antelope**
a colony of **ants**

B
a swarm of **bees**
a flock of **birds**

C
a caravan of **camels**
an army of **caterpillars**

D
a herd of **deer**
a pack, cry, or kennel
   of **dogs**

E
a parade of **elephants**

F
a shoal of **fish**
a swarm of **flies**

G
a herd of **goats**
a band of **gorillas**

H
a brood of **hens**

J
a fluther of **jellyfish**

K

a litter of **kittens**

a mob of **kangeroos**

L

A pride of **lions**

A plague of **locusts**

M

A labour of **moles**

A troop of **monkeys**

O

A parliament of **owls**

P

A string of **ponies**

A circus of **puffins**

R

A warren of **rabbits**

A pack of **rats**

S

A squabble of **seagulls**

A host of **sparrows**

T

an ambush or streak
of **tigers**

a knot of **toads**

V

a nest of **vipers**

W

a pod of **whales**

a pack or route of **wolves**

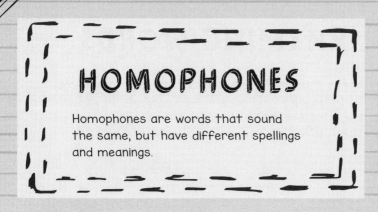

HOMOPHONES

Homophones are words that sound the same, but have different spellings and meanings.

aloud – allowed
bean – been
bored – board
by – bye – buy
cent – scent – sent
check – cheque
flour – flower
hire – higher
leak – leek
male – mail
new – knew
no – know
our – are
paw – poor

piece – peace
pore – poor
serial – cereal
site – sight
so – sew – sow
tail – tale
there – their – they're
through – threw
to – too – two
vain – vane
waist – waste
weak – week
weather – whether
we're – weir
where – wear

MY NOTES

RHYMING WORDS

Words that rhyme are words that sound the same. The rhyming sound is normally found at the end of the word. For example, 'gold' rhymes with 'old'.

-ain	-ice	-ock	-uck
• brain	• dice	• block	• chuck
• chain	• mice	• flock	• cluck
• gain	• nice	• knock	• pluck
• slain	• slice	• o'clock	• truck
• stain	• twice	• shock	• yuck

-ash	-ight	-oke
• bash	• bright	• awoke
• clash	• delight	• choke
• crash	• fright	• smoke
• lash	• might	• stroke
• smash	• sight	• woke

-est	-ill	-out
• best	• chill	• about
• chest	• fill	• scout
• crest	• skill	• shout
• pest	• spill	• snout
• quest	• thrill	• spout

8 My words and phrases

Stick your own lists of words and phrases in these pages, so that you've got all your writing ideas in one place.